THIS HORIZON

AND BEYOND

BOOKS BY NANCY-GAY ROTSTEIN

POETRY

Through the Eyes of a Woman   *(1975)*

Taking Off   *(1979)*

China: Shockwaves   *(1987)*

This Horizon and Beyond   *(2001)*

FICTION

Shattering Glass   *(1997)*

Nancy-Gay Rotstein

THIS HORIZON

AND BEYOND

Poems Selected and New

M&S

National Library of Canada Cataloguing in Publication Data

Rotstein, Nancy-Gay
This horizon and beyond : poems selected and new

ISBN 0-7710-7590-1

I. Title.

PS8585.O845T44 2001   C811'.54   C2001-930782-9
PR9199.3.R67T44 2001

We acknowledge the financial support of the Government of Canada through
the Book Publishing Industry Development Program for our publishing
activities. We further acknowledge the support of the Canada Council for the
Arts and the Ontario Arts Council for our publishing program.

Simultaneously published in Great Britain by Bellew Publishing Company Limited,
London; and in Australia by Brandl & Schlesinger Book Publishers, Sydney.

Printed and bound in Great Britain by Butler & Tanner Ltd.

McClelland & Stewart Ltd.
The Canadian Publishers
481 University Avenue
Toronto, Ontario
M5G 2E9
www.mcclelland.com

1 2 3 4 5   05 04 03 02 01

for Tracy, Marci and Stephen
for Max
and
in memory of Ida Berk

Contents

Sightings

Compass Points

EASTWARD

THE EQUINOX

The Cycle

Foreword
by Irving Layton

In this volume of selected and new poems (1975–2000), Nancy-Gay Rotstein's fourth volume, what comes across most clearly and emphatically to the reader is her choice of exact language. There is not a word that is superfluous. There is not a word that does not go straight for its mark and say what she wants it to say. Somehow or other she has a gift of isolating the manifold things and events experienced in one's daily life and of extracting from her observations and insights a broad, compelling vision.

What also is manifest is Rotstein's enjoyment of life – her enjoyment of what she hears, sees, tastes and touches. It is her heartfelt enjoyment of simply being alive. It's amazing how her eyes collect the significant item from the frothy muck that gives meaning to the rest. The world, all of life itself, may be a kind of mudscape – a lot of debris, a great deal of muck and rottenness – but her poet's sharp eyes detect the hidden diamond or pearl behind it or to the side of it. For her, the fact that her eyes catch that glimpse is of great significance. There is a great glinting somewhere, and her poems celebrate the enchantment and delight of that glinting. When I reviewed her first book *Through the Eyes of a Woman,* I said:

> Ms. Rotstein's poems give pleasure by their display of intelligence, sensitivity, compassion and warmth. Her ability to craft her observations into moving compositions and to confer significance on even the humdrum and familiar, surprises and delights again and again. Her eyes see clearly, and sometimes impishly, what others never see at all or don't wish to.

What time and experience have abundantly added is a quality of reflection. She sees things as they really are. She has the ability to see beyond or through appearances. Rotstein has put her living to good use; life has not been wasted on her.

Now and then she employs paradox, as in "Stages":

> *I can only warn danger*
> *wrap you in love*
> *and cheer, as you*
> *sinewed with dreams, stride*

She uses the unexpected paradoxical "sinewed." Now, who else but Rotstein would say "sinewed with dreams"? Dreams are what make many of us topple and fail and go astray; they are a weakening thing, not a strengthening thing. But they are to Rotstein, and that is consistent with her outlook and that is why unconsciously "sinewed" came into her mind.

In her poems about children, she watches them with a loving and caring eye. What impresses me is her realism, a nice warm human realism, and what I like most about Rotstein's poems is that there is a note of love, of caring, of affection. She is not a cold, analytical scientist but is involved in what she sees. "The Lesson" pretty well gives the reader her metaphysics, her outlook on life:

> *I take you with me*
> *as a heartbeat*
> *tucked inside my soul*
> *into the backstreets*

What I particularly like about her children's poems is the maternity they exhibit, a feeling of caring and warmth and the kind of insight that only love gives. It comes through love and no other way. That's what impresses me about her children's poems, her maternity in them. By maternity I mean the insight that comes through love. It's different from the insight of a philosopher or a theologian, but love has a kind of special way of looking at things and that's what Rotstein exhibits in these poems. They are true, they are authentic and avoid sentimentality. The great trap of writing poems about children is sentimentality. Well, she avoids that completely because her mind is working alongside her heart. They are working together. The other unusual thing about her children's poems is their universality. She has compressed all mothers' feelings about their progeny with an impressive freshness and vigour.

Rotstein's poems possess a hard, flinty, classical quality. She has the amazing ability to petrify her insights and observations into a hieroglyph, a statuary that will transcend the moment, that will transcend time. Though she has addressed herself to the times in which we live, she is no airy-fairy dreamer. She is able to give her observations the quality of a vase or a statue by a Renaissance artist, and make the temporal, the timely, into something transcendental and eternal, which is the aim of all great art. The artist is able to congeal the contradictions of life, its fluidities, and arrest the movement into eternal silence, thereby making decay impossible.

Rotstein's poems show her awareness of time and eternity and how they condition each other. Rotstein, like all enduring poets, is aware of the transcendental and eternal existing side by side, and how they condition each other to the eternal discomfort and perplexity of human beings.

Look at her wonderful poem "The Visitor." "I saw Alfred Dreyfus/at the Bagel Bar." She takes a figure from the past, Alfred Dreyfus, who lived in the last century, and situates him at a bagel bar:

> *his soldier-hands*
> *slowly stroking*
> *his bristled beard*
> *his eyes schooled*
> *in sadness.*
> *He sat on*
> *a tri-coloured chair*
> *a century-traveller*
> *unseen among*
> *the Sunday brunchers.*

Again, note the contrast. "A century-traveller/unseen among/the Sunday brunchers":

> *Unnoted, Dreyfus walks*
> *through the double-glass door*
> *and disappears.*
> *Tears pock his*
> *prison-pallored face,*
> *a ghost upon the*
> *haunted streets.*

Rotstein is evidently at home with history. To her, history is an old cloak which she puts on her shoulders and walks out in. It is the ease with which she makes these historical allusions that impresses me. There is no straining, no huffing and puffing.

Like many of Rotstein's other poems, "The Visitor" explodes with delicious irony and nuanced meanings.

— And here is another little gem I like very much, her poem "Marking Time":

His eyes once
piercing and aggressive
avoid another's gaze,
always resting somewhere
beyond, distant
as if searching
for the wife
forever young
frozen in memory
who splashed her life
desperately
upon the silent sidewalk.

You can hear the blood drops falling on the pavement.

Rotstein has the rare gift to see things as they are, the gift of the prophet. The prophets were not crystal gazers or readers of tea leaves who foretold events. Jeremiah and Amos were able to seize the temporal moment and the temporal event and foresee what the consequences would be. They were able to look at the corruption in Jerusalem and were able to foretell the fate of that doomed city. Rotstein appears to have the prophet's power to see deep into the nature of reality. The section "Sightings" exhibits her gift to see into the core of people and events. The last three lines of her poem "Power" say it all:

sophisticates of illusion
they have captured our world
and hold us all to ransom.

Inauthentic people, puffed up and arrogant with power, have captured our world today and they are the ones who "hold us all to ransom." I know no more disturbing and pertinent remark about the contemporary world than what I find in these three expressive lines.

Finally, Nancy-Gay Rotstein's poetry has a distinctive voice. It is not the kind of poetry written today, and that is very much in her favour. It gives to her poems a kind of hardness or toughness that makes for permanence, enabling her to take a lonely and significant place that is uniquely her own.

Sightings

Carousel

lithe Lippizaners leap
toward storybook stars
exposing golden hoofs,
sleek stallions spring
into frenzied silence,
centaurs carved for
Gepetto-chiselled perfect children
froth frozen foam

music pounds, centrifugal concave
calliope mirrors laughter

golden haired, the lady
sidesaddles gelding
and cradles the enlarged head
of her dreamy, droop-lid son,
fragile frame pressed secure;
his face, glowing,
is haunting in happiness;
her eyes are serene, carefree
as the crystal carousel spins

Remembrance Day

They place their wreaths
on stone steps
with practised dignity and empty faces
for sons, husbands, brothers;
faces alive in silvered frames
on cold mantels.
Young boys watch
awed by pomp and pageant
joyous with school recess,
unaware this tribal ritual
is part of the rite of spring.

Endangered Species

twilight, a weighted calm
fragrant and rushed with warmth

rhythmic, the gentle hulk rises and disappears
its sensual, silver skin shimmers
splits shoreward;
the mammal thrashes, twists opaque a violent froth
and resurfaces, alongside a frolic mate
to resume in mimic play, its paced loop arc

bloodless, rest the kill waters

circling, the scavenger spots the stilled place
and settles, rigid its matted midnight feathers
slope gullet quivers
sleuthful slits penetrate beneath
the benign patch
for after kill

but another creature
bloated with words and passion
nostrils filled with scent of sport
of spoil made too easy, too palatable
courts playmates of steel, grotesque bastard creations
legitimized, siloed, and waiting

will memories be burnt off the millennia of sand
and the cadenced sea silenced at birth?

Marking Time

He does not go
out anymore
his blue serge suit
folded carefully in
its tailor's case
waiting for the next
funeral or wedding.

His hand once
feared in battle
slowly strokes
his few stalks
of silver hair
and then slides
over the ridge
carved in Calais.
Another hand
(two fingers
severed by shrapnel)
absently fills his pipe
forcing each grain
still deeper into
its antique bowl.

His eyes once
piercing and aggressive
avoid another's gaze,
always resting somewhere
beyond, distant

as if searching
for the wife
forever young
frozen in memory
who splashed her life
desperately
upon the silent sidewalk.

Spring Fog

The mist shrouds the city
with its heavy stillness
blurring street lights and the cigarette
of the passing girl
whose soft chatter
echoes mercilessly
over vacant silence.
Encased in their homes
city hermits,
secure within this
silent grey garb,
listen once more
to the whimper of a heart.

The Reunion

you used to sit in
cloistered college room
on oversized Persian pillows
in sleek store jeans
encircled by dream posters
and fat foreign volumes
timbre silken
applauding Shaw and Greer
Schweitzer and Mansfield
boosting Mozart and Mathis
Reverend King and muscled fullbacks

now you sit opposite
a decade removed
behind chocolate almond cake
shawl dumped over marbled shoulders
voice raw
shunning convention deans, major papers
motherhood, marital ties
courting salary politics, chic eateries
motel encounters, lesbian liaisons
censoring memories,
editing potential

we separate at street crossing
paths rent
myself, an unwelcome mirror,
of choices

Homecoming

Strange children
run from familiar doors
immortalized by memories,
they scream
their two-wheelers into curbs
I once claimed as my own,
exchange bubble-gum cards
in my beloved bastion
under the garage extension;
even the houses look the same,
refusing my rescue.
I sit on the same hill
(too large to blend again
into those dandelions
bludgeoning the yawning green)
and envy the trees
who shed
their birth-skin, so easily
on the quiet lawn.

The Visitor

I saw Alfred Dreyfus
at the Bagel Bar
his soldier-hands
slowly stroking
his bristled beard
his eyes schooled
in sadness.
He sat on
a tri-coloured chair
a century-traveller
unseen among
the Sunday brunchers.

They arrive with
their children,
Cardin-dressed,
arms linked, laughing,
prosperous in their joy.
They greet their friends
exchange diet charts
talk of trips taken
and those yet to come.

Unnoted, Dreyfus walks
through the double-glass door
and disappears.
Tears pock his
prison-pallored face,
a ghost upon the
haunted streets.

Dossier

I am a Jew
I was born in the swirling sands of Sinai
when Moses descended the Mount.
I was driven from my home
by Roman decree
I prayed in *carceles*
with tortured men screaming round
I heard the chanting voices of children
in Dachau
I fled across oceans.
Again, tolerated for riches and illusive power
I dwell among strangers,
waiting.

Power

they tilt champagne
in padded boardrooms
and toast success,
they pop caviar
and collect for hunger,
at backgammon
they boast of bloodlines
disclaiming prejudice,
they prim for photos
their smiles
knitted by Scandinavian surgeons;
sophisticates of illusion
they have captured our world
and hold us all to ransom

Peace With Honour

Peace with honour,
voiceless lips shouting
vanity;
relieved faces
deprived of newsworthy atrocities
at family hour return to
documentary bloodletting;
dinner over, they consume
the carnage of Carthage
Culloden or Khartoum,
digest Caesar, Napoleon or Allenby
until Mars
in mutations of
Hobbes, Malthus and Nietzsche
calls them to avenge
their honour.

Recycled History

All things happen while the world sleeps.
Only lone eagles saw Hannibal
tame the Alps elephant trumphets ablare,
Archimedes jumping from experimental tub
attracted not the slightest stare
and it is just rumoured stars
fell at Caesar's birth –
most Romans were walking in the hot night air.
When David was born
only Michelangelo knew,
when Plato first taught
there was no milieu
and when oil-rigged sheiks slept
the four horsemen obediently left.

The Bat

Hair-pin toes fasten the
creature to the withered screen
wind-bellows bludgeon its sleeping shadow
the evening sun shoots
sharpened blood streaks
through its translucent frame
seeking its midnight heart.
La chauve-souris
limp in twilight's limbo
screen-sways,
its fat fuzzy head rocking.
Faceless children
with speared stakes
and piercing pencils
prod the dangling demagogue,
el murcielago's
black buttressed body
hangs suspended.

Bargain

I dance with demons
upon a jut of stone;
harnessed by furies
to twist in torment
and lured by ledgered taunts
until soul-forsaken, sightless,
I collide with death

The Master

The great man sat
rumpled, humble, exposed
teaching in a voice
siphoned from stars
of man, his frailties and hopes;
the uncommitted watched
brazen from wine and ignorance
they questioned, and as he spoke
silence shook the room.

The Victim

I am 30;
night news my bedtime,
children's noises tolerated 'til six,
laughter doesn't seem worth the wrinkles
or riding horses wise in winter.
People start to die
friends harder to make, circles narrow
rather than augment on fall days.
The road not taken
seems further in the distance;
and I, victim of the youth cult,
the unwilling traveller.

He

he declares home and family her responsibility
and expects no demands after the work day
In an age of self-expression
he condemns her interests as trivia
and picks her classes and clubs.
In an age of identity crisis
he asks what she does of importance
and concludes nothing.
In an age of shared decision-making
he demands sole control over spending
being the breadwinner.
In an age of transition
he wonders the reason for liberated woman
and boasts ignorance.

Stroke

How I used to fear her
this haughty, high-spirited lady
tall, arrogant, commanding;
now she stumbles into the room
legs propelling erect body,
eyes popping with frosty fear.
Not able to talk
she answers with shaky finger
urgently directing the beautician
on matters still deemed vital.
Seeing the metamorphosis
I tremble more now
searching for a flicker
a promise of life revitalized
for this tormented
caged creature.

The Age of Aquarius

They gave up on God;
inconsequential, they said
for their universe

They gave up on love;
replacing tenderness with
honesty
honesty enough to sting and
bruise the most trusting

and what's left –
indifference;
you can't get hung up on that
or live either

Greatness

FOR IRVING LAYTON

Great old bear
you fooled them all,
critics, interviewers
with your hauteur
and ripe illusions.
They dare not see
the soft eye lines
the gentle open hands
and certainly not the
heart
swollen and exposed
from caring.

Rummage Sale

Who shall claim you
for fifty cents?
A dealer
grabbing at forsaken limited editions
hoping his ignorance is not mirrored by others?
A student
sandwiching your book between
Chaucer and the *National Geographic*?
I must take you home
cherish you as my own
and guard the gentle words
that give you life.

Susan's Story

Alone, like a cavern
deep and unending, echoing
silence. No twinge of life,
no nerves throb
ever to hurt again.
Alone, only an abyss
where a heart had lived.

The brain endures, numbed with love
recalling plans half-formed,
dreams shattered.
Once touched by the gentlest of men
how can I turn to an empty embrace.

For me, all is emptiness.
My love, I follow.

The Choice

melancholy spring
seasons, mark a lifetime spent
in pursuit

I choose not the course
but a window
beside bursting ice-puzzles
and tulips,
pungent with birth
to defy the flame figures
that glow and die:
fuel for an ash winter

Decision

I feel your thoughts
the texture of seasons woven,
stroke birth from fox pups
hurled from earth womb;
hear grain slice black soil
breath sucked through thirsting stocks
gather sequins of rainbow skins
bathed in milk honey,
slide beneath cocoon of latticed lace;
and how to leave plans torn, dreams forgotten
for glistening cathedrals of mind-merchants?
I hear windmusic
and must dance upon crystal suntears

The Interview

over an interview, we strain
for matter that forms a story
the weaver of dreams and the hardened chronicler

her pen stops
"My daughter died last spring,
she wrote poetry, like you.
Beside her were found writings,
her need to explain a world
she did not wish to inhabit.
They thought murder
but I always knew she didn't belong here.
May I show you her picture?"
haunting eyes stare
from a portfolio of serene features

we part
I stumble into the common work-a-day world
and grab for the solid, the ordinary

The Bond

when we leave this world —
cheques, stubs
scrawls of wrenched dreams
for others to patch;
if they love us
they will reach and linger,
then discard
with only a final backward glance
to search for their dreams

The Race

I feel the wind
from Mercury's winged feet
cold on my raw back,
few good years left.
Not Herculean
no one will offer his life for ours.
We must reach out – touch
recreate our bond
tattered with distance's neglect
before Death, sure-footed and swift
silences our hearts.

The Legacy

When I die
build for me no memorial.
But if there be more
when all has passed
it's in a book or half-opened drawer;
there someone will find my image
etched on yellowed paper,
perhaps an idea affirmed
or truth yet to be learned;
for always, ideas are life.

Awareness

insects pound the night window
pulp their fine fabric
into the frantic search;
a light burns midnight
dark trees
silhouette an awesome scape

and I thrash
with promises not kept
faces I cannot touch;
pain numbs awareness
in my withering frame

a train whistle calls
someplace I shall never go

The Believer

chill, the distancing sun
wind-shadows
along a sweep of shore
the watery rattle

and a soul loosens

solitary the form
clamped at the salty edge
stares the unseen perimeter;
its night-shadow
grows a bony length
fine plumage disrobed;
trembling on skeleton stilts
unmasked and contrite
it faces the vacant wash
and nakedness restored
sentries feverishly
the constant cadence of stars

Compass Points

EASTWARD

[EDITOR'S NOTE: *Nancy-Gay Rotstein was one of the early foreigners to enter China after the Cultural Revolution. Invited on a special literary visa in 1980, she had extraordinary access and was granted the unique opportunity to explore places usually barred to foreign visitors. During her travels, she sensed a country undergoing change, and, as exemplified in her Foreword to* China: Shockwaves, *written nine years before the massacre in Tiananmen Square, she displayed a highly insightful predictive power. In that foreword she wrote, "The invited foreigner must not forget that he is entering a world in transition, a paradoxical world flirting with consumerism and private incentives while committed to doctrinaire idealism. ... The North American syndrome asserting privilege and demands is a luxury not permissible here, an acute illness capable of proliferating the malcontent twins of envy and greed. Ultimately, they can undermine relations and speed a return to retrenchment and dark silence."*

The selections that follow are all from China: Shockwaves, *beginning with those poems written while she was travelling with hundreds of villagers on a ferry for three and a half days down the Yangtze River and through the Gorges.*]

Yangtze River Gorges

I

I descend into Dante blackness
sweat bearers, poles harnessed to bone
stagger forms press into rust hull
shrills shriek as thick wash churns the crimson sea

I wake to raging sun:
spindle brush clump on belly hills
slashed falls sprout red syrup
birthing ruffle tiers
of sweet potato and cabbage, hand-sculptured
granite geometrics sheer into Yangtze
above snoozing *huo chuan*

we strap against Fu Lin's burdened side
hill queues clutter thousand dynasty blocks,
a weaving women processional of
wicker bushels, tubed pepper mustard
carcass rib braces ache across worn plank,
tea vendors barter with deck sleepers
over escape geese cacophony, rooster calls;
behind rails, military maidens flirt
a satchel woman snatches her child's hand

at midnight, we attach to Wan Xian's cliffs:
twinned sisters, placenta tied
share gleaming hunger eye, slash mouth, stench flesh
await dawn's gorge release

II

White King City's table gateway soars
above sudden swirls that throw me before
scrub mountains, footpath scarred into face
and hatched butcher veins
to release me onto satin wash;
primal peaks tower raw, exposed
as mist echoes enfold

in the distance, Twelve Peak
music canvas tinkles as lime splinters
tool cliff for hive kilns
goat miniatures wander on rock juts
above masked huts, puff swirl betrayed
and heavy toil chant rises
from galley oarsmen as ancient dugout
defies the dark churning current

sky peak dissolves sun
casts beacon light into opaque depths
myself, Tang helmsman
navigating between shroud mountains
foam precipice, whirlpool jettisoned by
shed dragon skin, tossed monster boulders
chill demon fury sears flesh

mountain boys probe for reptile primates
sunset slides across the worn universe

Glass Brothers

the aisle sleepers huddle window balustrade
their innocent hands grasp toward display delicacies
child eyes delight in white cloth, ivory napkins
step relatives carve rice wads,
desecrate picture food, sample fish rarities
ignoring glass brothers, hunger whites gleaming
swollen in twilight's cruel refraction

haunted eyes gobble
scarped fish skeleton, egg shreds
the cabbage remnants abandoned on crimson porcelain

complaint, they withdraw to rust corridors
and crusted rice bowls

East Is Red Steamer

I walk among debris:
masses strewn across tin belly
bodies line plank aisles
a human blanket
routinely scattered for privileged passage
to white cloth diner,
a mother presses baby, shielding
supple frame;
revolutionaries smile from iron walls
wary uniforms mark my interest
note-taking, feigned poster concentration
docile forms stir, uneasy

I escape below
machine perspiration, body stench merge
haunched basket woman knits
to speaker's eerie chant
of cadenced Jingle Bells
bandaged elder sits immobile
raw pipe drips, spills cold upon his face
youth soldiers joust makeshift checkers
ooze hostile looks

retreat through barrier mattress class
to observing parlour
from squash chairs sleek escape Chinese
returning step cousins
toss cards, munch import biscuits
as wrenched culture roots
unnoticed slide by

Wan Xian

belly strapped ferries
beacon lights
lock into mountain stars

I exit through vacuum hold, stench compartment
pig carcass' rot, sweat entrails
swing from rust crusting;
over sprawled aisle claimant
cradling his cackling possession;
up wash tiered steps
into Yangtze's midnight city

path disappears into seamen swollen
rice parlours of steaming vats
dangling pork, skewered duck;
a rooster kill displays
in gutter market
to circle of gnarled faces
delighting in white plumes
bloodstained on cobble;
fruit vendors haggle, tip
yellow pomelo on port-dipped scales;
cacophony of barter clatter, pressed confusion
lure me into fabled narrows

at dawn
pole carriers descend
endless slime stones
a silent processional,
wickers of green mandarins

rattan relay onto snoozing conveyor,
an aged support link
taunting China's ancestral sea

The Entrepreneur

collage photos doctored by herbal dyes
promote his recent sideline
as he charms with flowered tie
zoot suit with fat lapels
brazen from secret storage

his clients ruffle hair
rehearse smiles before polished metal reflector

he centres between
victory arch-span bridge, petal lights
flung above MacArthur's mud-puddle island
Yangtze's interminable flood delta
and throb from crimson factory hills

avoiding the Ancient
satiated by oblivion's rotting dream pipe

Chungking Incursion

Asian bone roaches shred
filament grease curtains
in frenzy hunger search
vanishing in black spit pots,
an ancient haunches against
rotting corridor blocks
transported into lotus visions
opium pipe nods fray chin wisps

sidewalk hordes stare, consuming
homosapien curios, rare variety
Marco Polo oddities –
leering faces, eight-deep circle
ensnare in humanity compressor,
squeeze blanched flesh,
ancient swings skewered chicken
another examines caged duck specimen
goose trapped in bamboo basket

sole foreigners on unexpected intrusion
a delicacy import

The Gathering

they walk through yellow waves
with sickle staffs and wicker bushels
to claim the golden harvest
families slice root with swift base thrusts
deserting thick stubs to soft slog
teams wrist flick, foot crank –
sheaths spit from ancient gobbler
into sheltered refuge, branch discard
swiftly tied, twine-bound
a mother snatches mud toddler
from machine mouth

paddle whine blankets field girls
rising cadence
granny, searching for lost solitary stocks
bends among a tassel sea
reliefed by soaring tabernacle peak

Tiananmen Square

wheels, endless wheels
churning Tiananmen's evening dust mist
resolute faces compress into
swollen blue accordions
blurred cyclists, epoch spinners
press by red-star army child
unafraid with blond stranger
youths touch

across square, unsealed Forbidden City
with ancestral guardians
pressure spokes prod anaesthetized dragon
its dry flame tongue flexing

Impasse

I speed along fresh pavement
masked sweepers massage its dust shoulders
aging figures pedicure shrub
balance debris satchels, waiting human harness

bulldozers crack the good earth's parched crust
a blue uniform constructs
gold-fired geometrics one by one
onto bicycle slab, then pedals away
paced convoy donkey jostles sleeping chaperone

in chunked progression
numbered cement rises opposite
the crumbling mud compounds
interlocking feudal huts
labyrinthed by pitted earth
open on excrement ditch, sewage-wash

stucco horns counterpoint the cyclists' bells
Flying Pigeons transport thrashing ducks
the slashed goat bleeds, billboard stereos bleat
and the master expressway
a gaping cloverleaf impasse
expresses an awakening China

Great Hall of the People

alone, in auditorium
among padded seats, dialect phones
I face vacuum chairman stage

imported tourist streams
rave of reception filigree
peacock-blossom porcelain
embroidered screen, vibrancy
of Taiwan room's reclaiming mural;
a child-cadre follows
Young Pioneers grip school packs
rooted in awed obedience

in gaping arena, a double alien,
I watch the crimson star radiate
its vortex pulse

Visit to Thirteenth Middle School

the principal and chief teacher attend
my passage through decayed corridors
whispered lessons gape through ventilation,
window confessors

beneath benevolent father twins, emptied bookshelves
I take my prescribed guest seat

under raw string fluorescents, the instructor extracts
a replay excellence of ideological parsing

a bell rings – programmed eye exercises:
muscles gyrate to cadenced ancestor music,
dismissed into student delight,
girls link fingers, boys hug and laugh

at a silent signal
the eager, animated mass
transforms into an avid corps
perfects drill-squad manoeuvres
executes precision war-pack running
with ferocity and enthusiasm

afterward, the robots dissolve again
into smiles, touching, neck embraces
and I am left to ponder
which seedling personality
we will permit to survive

Block Captain

she rules her numbered cement city
with frozen resolution
she dictates marriage and divorce
living-space rewards

she guides random apartment tour –
music, incense, focal Canadian calendar –
exhibiting her created neighbourhood,
the production of women elders
coughing in chill-slab jade workrooms

her commandant face boasts
a slash-smile

The Great Wall of China

wind twilight
swirls down dragon backside
hurling me into ghosts of wall toilers
bones crushed into debris siding
confronting warring history
soldier colonies, shadow glow
of beacon's tower alarm
echo of carriage horses

spanning desert to sea, undulating protector

here entourage politicians
pose for videos
invade with impunity

flank culture defences, silently

The Ambassador to Beijing

alone at Cinderella hour
I enter the emptied enclave;
the ambassador oozes
bourbon and charm
acquired from Continental trysts

his wife, a trophy from other postings,
waits in chill museum salon,
porcelain among rare collectibles;
her eyes brighten at gift
of dated journals and texts

he tears at taped pouch,
yearns for news of distant friends
and truth snatches,
mixes lovers, honours, literature
with decanters of Cointreau

the heater sputters
forsakes the frost room
and aging statesman
desperate
in the constraint of China

Foreign Concessions, 1980s

I sit among Czar alabaster columns
Greek tassel lamps

a room of ambassadors
in Babel clatter

executive reprints,
Wall Street Japanese
tilt rubbed ivory
over vested delicacies,
escrow pocket condiments

micro-chip Koreans
with swollen computer cases
mechanic satchels,
roll polyester sleeves,
their rice bowls suspended

comrade legates relish
privilege abundance,
dangling of coiffured
foreign beauty's
loop gold earrings

shrouded in black cigar Lebanese,
corporate diplomats
meticulous in menu Mandarin
jockey and spin again
in their concentric islands

Ming Tombs

in chill tomb heart
they display canvas sham
didactic mist mockery
pseudo master craft
with mind-fermenting script

the comrades press into airless tube
for their session with Ming abuses,
revengeful peasant contempt;
tyranny graphs, bloated statistics
glare from moist blocks;
they emerge into the clear sunshine
redeemed, contemplative

the angered child
hurls his slingshot
at the privilege limousine
exiting the dust garden
and leaving behind the glazed dragons

China Trader

strangers pulsing through Pacific sky
talking till day became night
to return
talking as silent frames
leap from pin-projectiles,
to dissolve –
talking as suckled infants cry again
into gastric awareness

of grandfather-trader
pampered in foreign concessions
by respect-raped Chinese –
cloistered enclaves, swollen banquets
cloying opulence, gorbelly corruption
aunt dancing into Sun's fading flare

of his own legacied return,
merchant mercenary, dispassioned chronicler
he watched, while oxygen deprived
slashed into Caesarean consciousness
she writhed in bloody afterbirth

Lake Tai Images

mist dragon
with silk wind vapour, sweat phantoms
slips from Louyang to Hanchow
helmed by canal-emperor's will

red-scarfed Pioneers burst into
wood slab barge for reward outing
circling willow nurseries
white bait hatcheries' silvered translucents
webbed oyster harbours;
nesting bamboo shells clog sludge canals;
beside island, fisherman buckets water
into pirate weed camouflage,
draws barren net into flat hull
to mud rhythm from polling barefoot child
woman sprawls boat wash
across tarp sky;
tuo chuan groan under toil processional
dwarfed by tung oil's black fan
haunting monster specter;
animal peak, ruptured from Tai's stone belly
flares twilight jagged

Yang Di, emperor during the Sui dynasty, linked three sections of the Grand Canal. He was the first person to sail down the completed canal.

Xing Guo Guest House, Shanghai

I lie on embroidered crisp sheets
amid carved trunk lacquer
room yawning into room of silken heirloom rugs,
rubbed oak, Empire-splendour chandeliers;
from fat screened veranda, a misted English garden.

I remember cursed enclaves
cries of rapier concessions, rabid privilege;
now reinforced metal gate barricades
roadside cabbage decay, factory script boasts,
sheltered legations.
                        Honoured envoys again sleep
in transplant Suffolk estate behind walls
cloistered from commitment, Chinese dignity
a neo-colonial apparition.

Overnight in Shanghai

I walk Shanghai's rib
rub bodies, inhale stale breath
of compressed humanity,
crushed in flesh tide

they claim Non Jing Dong
scorn sedan's incessive defence pleas
gape its privileged passengers,
flaunt amplified threats
from sheltered dais police
immobile colonial relics;
disbelievers huddle gyrating Seiko display
motile magician windows,
glut vintage movie houses

flash clothes with worker blue
accordion transport among pedicabs
cranes underpinned by bamboo

at dawn
florid track-suited youths
jog past *Tai ji quan*
stationary elders

Commune Visits

officials greet my scheduled arrival
cloud tea, to rote of commune statistics
private incentives, growth projectiles
precisely interpreter translated;
music path lures to chosen random hut
soft bed, fat pillows, charm resident
and sculpture vegetable beds with mammoth greens,
swirl fish ponds, scrubbed swine pen
Polaroid snap, sugar gum, yuan expected

an unofficial detour,
I follow smudge wire-hoop host
along paddy divide
past oxen, ancient sunk harness deep
among sludge eels
boy scrubbing in mud moss
into seedling courtyard:
barefoot toddlers behind
a pied-piper coterie;
hens dine at bloated potato leaf mounds,
elder squats, scrapes lotus root
inside swine-odour entrance,
sorghum stacks dry against chip-rock frame
garden toiler splatters hoarded human manure
goitered ancient gnaws sweet potato
toddlers cringe from sweets,
hide from instant chronicler

at car's retreat
signal mud boy reappears
skips metal loop down paddy path

As If They Had Never Been

they heard of Buddhist
Taoist, Muslims
not Jews
especially not Shanghai Jews
who swelled the scourge-Bund
then fled
with skullcap and silver candles
terror replacing terror

no synagogue or marker
no script character or swatch-allophone
no youth memory

erased
as rice wind

English Teacher
Foreign Language Institute, Shanghai

we met on Guilin's river journey
her cane thrust at superlatives
in German, English, Chinese
a quarter-century Shanghai teacher
herself a first time tourist
permitted traveller

we meet alone over lunch
Chinese husband absent
conversation starved, unafraid
she speaks of outwitting
interracial love in Fatherland
enduring Mao's confinement
of engineer spouse;
she speaks of not belonging
of sand-roots, straining
of recent German pilgrimage
identity search
unexpected alien reaction, self-isolation:
aging history survivor, lost

View from Catching Cloud
Pavilion, Guilin

I voyage through caves of dragon teeth
wind chambers protected by stelae and charm poems
to spinning earth table, tied to crystal cloud

below, pulsing China microcosm
a dust city of wicker sweepers, soft sedans
human yolk carts, levered cranes;
farmscape of sludge oxen, straw mud toilers
pedicured communes, nurtured fish hatcheries;
Li River *chuan* life of
patched tarp families, sweat drag harness
upstream motor launch
disciplined Young Pioneers snatch laughter

a soldier tirelessly scribes praise poems
by Zhu De, Xu Te-li
frocked girls smile, proffer me green mandarins
tenuously

peaks rise from granite crag

Li River Cruise

visitors stream onto Li River's flotilla
prepared with packaged tables of candies
sliding windows, hot galley service
groups unfurl mandarins as dream magic turns
caves to moon craters, hills to curled lotus petals
as playful dragons, painted horses, bull horns
leap from rock illusion
to dissolve again into granite indifference
sun chatterers stretch topside
pack women sling silken *ma* bundles
along thirsting bank
others swirl greens from mud plank
steaming *chuan* village hides,
clusters nuzzle into cave sanctuary
buffalo douse in cool liquid
bow horns locked in mud delight
harness child toils cargo *shanban*
across pebble siding
clan hunter releases cormorant spear
as travellers return for chicken banquet
save aged Shanghai teacher, China adoptee
sensing each lime shading, life realism

and always those peaks
those tablet peaks, silent

Aftershock

I cannot adapt to this world
of proffered elegance
of velveteen chairs, bribed kindness, gold toadyism
have I changed
or skin stripped from cataract eyes?

I am haunted by a purpose society
from atrophy and chaos
salvaging intellect
from cold, blistering concrete
restoring pride
from harness paddies, body waste
gifting life
from aged gleaners, dust sweepers
toiling respect
from bamboo and crimson clay
forming dreams

while we, lotus-eaters
consumer mandarins
swirl in monied frenzy
and pleasure analysis

Hong Kong, 1980

Hong Kong Skyline

rigid concrete cubes
geometric reprints
amoeba sprawl, extrude
into compressed mechano skyline,
zip trams, speed ferries, bullet buses
pace traders, shop merchants,
compete elongated hours
robber baron ambitions under Asian smiles

tattered card dwellings
thrown from squatter cliffs
balance on spindle legs in mountain clusters
corrugated soiled decks – stained complements;
Aberdeen junks strain for air shine
salt gnaws engorged bellies
sterns trestle in poverty subdivision
of pork limbs, skeleton fish, torn web nets

an allogenic fusion
of flipped tailpipe
appended to a writhing dragon body

Peninsula Lobby

I watch merchant princes
swing D'Oyly Carte doors
swashed by miniature sailors
balancing pillbox caps

Asian compatriots sit
at *petit four* war table
redefine stratagems
with linguistic fervour
plot market invasion
(finished textiles only)

nanny prims on Viennese brothel seat
beside knickered charges

courting Saks buyer
Australian female designate
mingle season fabric-swatch snippings
with velvet aperitifs and satin glances
beneath laughing plastic masks
and classical flutings

Japanese business clones team
Arab ally-adversaries
demand statistics, instant projections
over lobby clatter, page jangle, dish chatter
assert with ivory smiles and scraping civility
to elicit hypnotic compliance

front desk steward anticipates
lush entrance of poised Asian exquisites,
naval cut-outs again
open polished doors to commerce boudoir

From Victoria Peak

I

from Victoria Peak
granite spirals in Pisa illusion
above divided city-harbour,
Kowloon ferry peninsula stretches
toward mythical Asian raft
a retracting, drugged guardian

II

I propel with crowd pace
as fashion employees speed walk,
press shops, restaurants for today's indulgence
in clothes banquets, disco feasts, food swilling
payable in levered salaries, penny stock rolls;
savings purged, their banks recycle money
for Voltaire chess players, continent jockeys;
choreographed ballet cranes swing
with free market rhythm –
built from gold dust, sold for futures

all caught in the cabaret frenzy
of an abbreviated future

Hong Kong, 1980

THE EQUINOX

Columbia Icefields

I stand at the foothills:
a scar on albino skin
encased by towering
granite-stained craters
chiselled from green ice.
Wind sears my ears
sun screams birth
to burning sockets,
tears off my skin
in a blaze of cold
creating

and always the ice,
that wilderness of ice,
churning.

Farm Winter

Cold sun warms
mid-season snow
its colours refracting
rivulets of water
into the churning creek.
Horses wearing
winter-thick coats
stamp stable floors
waiting for fodder.
Red spots splashed
on winter-white skin,
Ayrshires munch alfalfa
in solitary stalls.

From the distance
a yard-gate groans,
wind pushing its
tired timber to-and-fro
its arms encircling
emptiness.

Images in Snow

I am the first wanderer
in this wilderness of snow,
Moses in a snow desert.
My step breaks
the frozen silence
as my feet sink slowly
into the powdered softness.
The cold sun strikes
the oasis-trees
transforming knife icicles
into a flame;
the sand-wind whips
my uncovered face
forcing each pore
open, vibrant, alive.

Winter Ride

I ride a whirlwind
round a circle
rocking as one,
knees locked
into shoulder,
chestnut sides
shining with sweat.

Ice-snow slams
against steel shed
pigeons panic
jump from post to post
winter birds
fall as bullets
into sinking sod,
scratching for seed.

A universe
moving as one
its centre the
earth's core,
Sisyphus
upon a horse
forever circling
frozen in frenzied time.

View from a Hill

Snow spreads below,
skidoo and ski tracks
scratch their long
white fingers
across its albino
skin, scarring
its perfect face.
Tree statues
stand empty,
their arms
stripped bare
raised against
the grey sky.
A train whistle's
wail echoes over
this vast emptiness,
a prisoner in solitude.

Awakening

Mud oozes under
black boots claiming
fly-away fodder;
feed, freed from
winter storage
shores up stable door.
Spiles stab maple
trees, releasing
sweet syrup
into plastic pipes;
burnt smell of
boiling sap
mingles with embryo
sweetness of spring.
Birch trees stripped
of snow's camouflage
become virgin pillars
proud against blue sky;
bird-flocks attack
the air, making wild patterns,
robins reclaim
abandoned alcoves,
rivers surge with
embryotic run-off.
Tractors tear the earth:
a Caesarean slash
heralding birth.

City Spring

The world is alive again.
Grass thaws into green lettuce
sun spins into radishes
tulips trade blackness
for acrylic life.
Children hopscotch to school
dripping chocolate cones
down no-iron tops.
A zoo elephant lifts
silvered trunk, and trumpets.

Northern Morning

Morning haze lightens
this gabled room
of canopy bed,
homespun wool
flowered paper
with lilac perfume.
Brass spittoon,
map of 1874
blue washstand
on latticed cloth,
soft feet touch
rough planked floor.
Peering through
patched attic window
I see ...
grain,
fields and fields
shifting golden ocean
breaking over a barn
by Van Gogh
far in the yellow distance.
Through patched attic window
I see
Ontario.

Exile

I saw you pause
air suspended, legs poised
in your Hapsburg hall –
columned gallery, coffered ceiling
Grecian gable plenteous of genei,
with ambassador handmaidens
and princely assistants –
Quadrille Empress led;
watched your perfect figures
cut with precision imposed
by generations of generals
under discipline of nobled masters
executed to Mozart and Strauss

I saw your stallion-leap again
on steamy airless noon of Ontario town
in carnie, acrylic flag-festooned arena
strong of cattle stench
attended by abandoned cottage children
and village transients;
your regal entrance balanced
between plastic-crowned pillars
piaffe scored to squashed
sugar cans' pop, chips' stale crunch
proud lineage seared
into white thigh-flesh
deposed dynasty

Siren's Lure

The cold crystalline lake
chants its icy clear call
as it catpaws past me.
Tree handmaidens,
summer leaves bulging
like swollen green balloons,
wave their farewell
as pixie sun-clouds
pluck their cloak from
lime to evergreen.

How I wish to drift
from this shaky summer dock
and follow your siren's song
as it echoes into the languid Ottawa
luring me past
beaver runs, salmon-springs
and deer nurtured by your
now stilled frosty cup,
and like them taste eagerly
your turbulence and compassion.

The Swimmer

I skim along surface
pulled by invisible string,
below
bushes and boulders
magnify, fingers elongate

swim-hands strain
to reach sun,
fall again
into stilled mirror stream,
leaving but a fleeting legacy

of breath-bubbles

Canadian Paradox

Water and sky join in
summer's hazed stillness
over land still adolescent
from unprotected conception.

White butterfly wings jumping
over sweet morning grass
quiet the speeding
foreign-pipeline truck.

Melodies from city children
exploring mouldering woodland
rise in *la langue*
to rouse a sleeping country.

Shanty Bay, 1975

From North Bay

I saw the last plane leave.
The flag continues to flap
its red and white linen
over the barren turf,
black fly buzzing
replaces the retreating turbos.
My love, they left you
exposed and forgotten.

The Conquerors

The flagged charger
lunges through the water
gauging its acrylic sheen
with mangled metal
till white tail-wash
bloodies its pure blue cape.
Birds screech from sheltering sky
beavers slam fat tails
and dive for wooded dam.

Do not fear us
future's emissary:
we bring only
whale-bone rods,
cat-gut cord with
sharpened spears
and lures of steel.

The Deer

I met you first
beside the river,
melting alive,
your grey-faced fawn
safe behind
swabbed by evergreen.
Your coat was winter-matted
eyes soft, secure,
head cocked with wonder.

I saw you again.
Your coat shining
in silvered perfection
eyes wide, glassy,
head hanging lifeless
on hunter's cold mantel.

The Wrecking

I saw the old place come down.
After one hit
it began to heave.
Another hit and it spilled
its guts on the living room floor.

There isn't much left, they said
just some Tudor beams
pillars and carved railing.
But they soon took those away too.

When they came to level the ground
they said it seemed a shame
but the home was in the way.
Now graded powder scatters
in the grey wind, betrayed.

Site Plan for Subdivision A

Answer me
          with the lilt of trees or
                              drifting grey
          on a cloud-filled day.
Warn
     wandering beavers not to fear
     the cocked surveyor's transit or
     nesting birds
                    the henchman's grey blade.
Tell
    squirrels not to quaver
    at the lumbering sounds of
                              birth.
Only when wind-whispers
are caught on Muzak and
thickening clouds texture designer's
thoughts, will there be
                    progress.
Answer me
          with the lilt of trees or
                              drifting grey
          on a cloud-filled day.

Tuesday's Rape

We planted the seedling vine
nurtured it
until it covered that glistening metal wire
and made us forget about trees
pulled down for hydro.
Then came five brave leather-jacketed men
riding a municipal-lettered van,
helmeted, vine-pruner in hand.
Four cheered support
while their champion ascended the pole
beside the winter-brittle bush and
emasculated it
leaving short brown stubs.
Decayed wires glare in the damp hung air.

Waste

Between white streaked lines
exhaust fumes pant clear
in cold northern dawn;
the cars begin their tombed processional
into the dying city.

Grey industrial monuments jet-stream
into poisons spewed
from buses and factory machines;
a sooty pigeon's gurgle
paces the wrecker's ball.

Men, their faces emaciated, wait
in cubed office areas
distinguished by foreign plant species,
'til Friday.

Visit to the Ottawa

From the hill I see the virgin pine
rise from its earth-cradle
and stand pitted against the sky.

I am the first Algonquin
                              to wander here
and shout for his tribe to follow.

I am the first lumber baron
to stumble on this clearing,
                              pause
and wave his men away.

I am the first settler
                              to carve a cabin
at the edge of this valley.

I am a dweller
                    from the soul-lost city
permitted a weekend
                              and I cannot leave.

Days of Sunshine

evening breathes cold
on sun–lit hours
leaves hint of colour
the lake chills

I snatch the remnant
of the day
strive to press into it a summer's living
beauty bypassed, senses squandered
in the clamour of obligations
treasures abundant time never compelled
and plead futilely
as one unprepared in the final hour,
for moments more

Autumn

She departs slowly
swollen boughs reaching
to catch retreating red raiment.
Weak even at noon's nearness,
her breath tightens at twilight
with crisp cold gasps,
echoing over empty fields
stripped of steamy fullness.
Stumbling, she splashes
her palette
on the sleeping world.

BORDERS

While New York Burns

Perfect green, clear water
gentle waves licking sand
thrusting soft bubbles on adoring shore.
Perfect peace.
Creole, African, Spanish
lives entwined like Piamienco.
Harimento.

*Piamienco: colloquial for Papiamento, the language of Aruba; a blend of Creole,
African, Spanish, Dutch, Portuguese languages*

Harimento: "laughing"

Sint Maarten / St. Martin

Don't tell me your name
island goddess
or that of your
green coral-rimmed suitor
whose white hands wash
your brown belly
again and again;
your cliffs have
sheared many ships
my Siren maid,
made men mad
with your timeless peace
your solitude;
now my schizophrenic beauty
the iron birds
drop their burden
on your aching runways.

I'm Alive Again

I'm alive again
the splash of cold green water
the bite of ocean salt
brought me to life
after the dank city,
heavy clothes hiding
garbed souls
behind tri-locked doors
in cold sun-days
ever striving to be more
than a mis-spelt computer card.
The wind-sand rises
and whips my flesh.
I'm alive again,
for a week.

Dawn

Sun
midwife of the new day
hovers over the sea
languid from her sleepless night.
Gulls circle near
screeching their tribute.
A fishing boat cuts
into the open sea,
eager.

Earthquake

I was only sixteen.
The ocean lay
like a moss pond
life-filled and still,
stars frozen to
the Mexican sky.
Round hills ringed the water
where I stood
a lonely sand-speck,
knowing, sensing.

Tremors.
Darkness, fear echoing
over the ocean's calm,
and only the light of David
to guide.

Meaning

So high, the hills are moss-covered
carved with donkey trails
dark carvings against blue backdrop,
ocean pencils its life
along schoolboy bays,
figures move as miniatures
on chessboards
mindless pawns of humanity.
Island glaciers mirage my memory
of four-dimensional time
as I slip between them
weightless.

Bon Voyage

The ship savours its fortnight curtain call
past the high-rise and tinselled flags
    horns hoot, whistles wail;
flattered, she offers three encores and
    a puff of smoke.
Balloons burst, a siren intrudes
    from somewhere down the beach,
tennis balls continue their ceaseless whine.
Swirling white foam signals her farewell
    the cacophony ceases;
the sand, deserted, looks like squashed ice cream.

Disneyworld, U.S.A.

spiff-spangled brass bands
slash the silence, dislodging
overnight loitering sparrows
Polaroid-posing horses pull
painted tri-decked trollies
enamel fire engines race
to Peter Pan emergencies
steam engine's solitary
smoke-swirl signals Main Station
corn husks bubbling
in flowered antique bowls, burst
scattering its sweetness

chimes clang welcome as
wide-eyed wandering children
babies snug in shiny strollers
parent-pushed wheelchairs
and cane-assisted elders
stream down Main Street
to affirm for a day
their Disney dream of America

Bermuda

White limestone roofs
disappear into tourist-
demanded skies
roads curve
for postcard-courtesy
coral washes
picture-pink;
sharks refuse to bite
or jellyfish invade.
British properly protect
with white uniforms
and bare kneecaps,
radio announces
cricket scores and
other world events
with thick-accented
enthusiasm.

Strikes outlawed
union demands
ignored again
governor
India-inspired
sits in painted pink
house behind
hibiscus hidden walls,
napping.

Bermuda, 1978

The Predator

Wings suspended in solitude
the bird wielded its gorgon's head
scanning the curled surf, waiting
waiting for the bounty of Neptune's table.

A wave smashes it on coral;
white foam bubbling through matted feathers
on some lonely stretch of sand,
with broken wing, it waits.

Elegy for a Starfish

You glide sand smooth
life-filled fingers
pulsing and exposed.
I will not seize your
starbust trophy
to dismember, cure
until sucked free
of all save skin you lie
limp victim of a vulture's prey.

Not ego-infected
I will not jet-stream
your wasted tentacles
to caisson cubicle
to be admired
politely by dinner guests
or poked suspiciously
by children's friends.
Do not fear me, you are safe
until the next plane
brings a warrior,
lusting.

St. John

I study your history
lounge in cool green water
love in gardenia-scented gardens.

Awake at night, I hear the
moan of men grinding sugar
the ghost-scream of owners
spilling blood on Virgin soil
and the wind's ceaseless chant
of free men hurling
themselves upon brutal
boulders below.
I hear your anguish
and remember.

St. John, Virgin Islands, the scene of the slave rebellion of 1733

Journey's End

I suck strength
from your agelessness
from abandoned alcoves
of salt-blackened coral
shorn by swirling madness.
Only you know I am here
fastened on your blue back
weightless
time-torn as Odysseus
my travels suspended.

Port of Piraeus, Greece

Cargo carriers slash
the sea with steel
tugboats tear the silence
tankers defecate crude

where stood wooden ships
with white starched sails
and towering timber masts
searching for tool-metals
and gold for patient Phidias.

Now Themistocles,
Salamis-sailor, stands
with plumed helmet
one hand straining on sword,
another stretching seaward

with always the eyes
those eyes
resting sternly, somewhere
beyond.

City-State, 1978

Bunched blue buses
routinely rotate
through Syntagma Square
multitudes pinned
against pinched doors,
girls grasping steel straps.

Triple-tiered
billboards splash
the subconscious
selling diapers and dancers
airplanes and antiques.

Apartments assault
the senses stabbing
the Pantheon sky,
concrete replacing
Corinthian columns.

Political slogans
slashed red
glare from granite walls
beside graffito Byron-old,
scrawl across Poseidon's
scorched Sounion stone.

Kingdom of Mycenae

Agamemnon I come
to your Cyclopean court
passing Atreus' treasury
hidden high in Argas hills,
olive and orange orchards
ripening in valley sun.

I climb up
primal pathways
of cobbled marble
over rock-royal ramp,
palace protected with
monster stones adorned
by propylon pillars
carved high on
wind-whipped parapet.

Now the wind
grinds savage stones
over abandoned empire,
affirming Cassandra's
warnings.

Elounda Night

The sky is laced
with lanterns
a Pantheon universe
above ancients' Aegean
traversing time.

Hill houses festooned
with strings of
festive sparklers
become a lighted procession
spiralling upward
to Mt. Sitia.

Steamer signal scans
volcanic coast,
Ulysses lost upon
a trackless sea.

Cretan Fisherman

His skiff moves slowly
pulled by centuries
to secret spots
through silent sea
of the sacred Aegean.

He lowers his hand-line
back bent
a monastic montage
swabbed in weathered white
set against
stark peaks of
the Sitian hills.

He rows homeward
catch full
heat-haze
hiding him in
a steaming solitude.

Temple of Poseidon
at Cape Sounion

Transported through time
I stand upon
Poseidon's promontory
stones thrust toward sky
pillars scaped to stars.

I see Theseus'
black-sailed ship
hear Aegeans' anguished
sobs scream from
barren boulders
as wind-wails carry
a father's passion.

Sun-fire ignites
stone as
Poseidon again
claims the sea.

Prayer in Distomon

GOD ASKS THE PEOPLE
FOR EVERYONE TO WORK
HARD ON BELIEVING IN
HIM SO THAT THOSE PEOPLE
WILL LIVE IN PARADISE

Here families were
massacred, machine-gunned,
then throats gashed
by Nazi knives
slit on church steps –
priests, parents with sons
bones stored for
mass-mountain burial.
Nikolaou, Nikou, Ntae
names chiselled in
marble-blood plaque
placed below prayer.

Café chairs stand empty
deserted by town and tourist
severed from life.
Church bells chime
tortured hours,
a sole woman
black-clad
swiftly passes
the silent square.

Malpensa, Italy

Bags roll off rotary,
duffles bulging, battered, broken
box-cases bound with
twine and tape
soiled from service years;
elders wearing thread-thin
Sunday suits
exchange embraces.

Grey uniformed
marshalled men,
boots heavy on stone steps
survey square room;
one's hand on holstered gun,
the other, holding chain
of German shepherds
eager and attack-trained.

Relatives rush gate
grasp *famiglia*
squeeze poly-prim
children known only
by Christmas photos
then leave
animated, into the night.

Malpensa: International Airport near Milan

Escorted Inclusive Tour

They enter eating area
scheduled for breakfast,
saving stools for
new-found friends,
decisively refusing others.
They plant purses on
tabletops, reserving places,
a woman rejected
sits alone, smiling
expectantly at newcomers.
They proceed with precision
to half-board, hoarding
platterfuls of eggs and pastry
pushing yellowing
pictures of grandchildren.
Two men manufacture conversation;
another, alone, forgoes
buffet-seconds, afraid
to sacrifice seat.
Instructed tabletime over
they rush to restrooms
step upon air-conditioned bus
waiting
for today's excursion.

The Grand Hotel Villa D'Este

I walk among
platano trees
proud with age,
through Cernobbio
homes protected by
century-old *coppi,*
into a past
punctuated with
dreams and intrigue.

Here grew Elysian
gardens, graced by
a ballerina's hands
and buttresses where
mock military battles
amused a handsome husband.
Tears of royal Caroline
still dampen dark corridors,
while silhouette-shadows
whisper of Risorgimento and
gunfire echoes from Dongo
over a collapsed continent.

The Garrovo stream
spills into Como,
homes still hide
in hospice-hills,
tessitori spin
their subtle tapestry.

Dongo: town on Lake Como where Mussolini was executed

tessitori: "weavers"

Moods (from a balcony)

I / DAWN

mist:
a steaming white blanket
pulled over dawn's
sleeping hospice-hills
seals balcony,
aliscafi whisks into haze;
nestled in nearby alcoves
birds banter bravely,
San Giuseppe's spire
soars above cloud camouflaged flagpole,
sailboats disappear

Bisbino's beacon scans
silent sky, searching

II / NOON

a white silk-screened mask,
the heat rises
to trace the virgin hills:
wind lost sailboats stall
in steeping noon sun;
oarsman's face refracts
in stillborn stream;
balcony birds snooze
under sycamore's shade
and the red draped family flag
droops

its century crest
wilting

suspended above Bisbino hills,
the heat-haze slices
a rainbow ribbon:
hang-gliders hover above
Como's twilight currents and soar;
the wind snatches florid sheaths,
wind surfers swerve,
their tottering sails captured;
sailboats bob and tear at tether;
a balcony bird disappears
with twirl dropped
from honeyed croissant delight

Cernobbio church chimes
century-hours, eternal

Outdoor Tea-Time

White-coated men
with black bowties
precisely place
pastries and coffee
on silver serving trays,
expose each cup-crest
each starched napkin,
display European-emblem
embroidered cloths.

Arriving from world's
four corners, speaking
many tongues
they swarm to
sandwich table
ravage raspberry rolls
infest coffee with
sugar and cream

then disappear,
leaving a legacy
of stains and spills.
White-coated men
reappear, rearrange
barren tables
strip soiled cloths,
returning all to
silence and the sea.

Gandria Morning

Women stand timeless
in shuttered windows
framed by
Florentine fresco,
homes chiselled
with centuries' scalpel
into the Gandrian
cliffs, roofs baked
with coral *coppi.*
Cobblestone-slanted
streets twist through
ancient alleys;
sassifraga and edera
grow through
ravaged rock.
Watching approaching
aliscafi,
women shut shutters
hurry to restaurant or shop
ready for today's tourists.

Lake Scene

Blevio villas slice
into Bisbino hills,
brown gingerbread homes
with coral toppings.
A cotton-candy cloud
rings the crest
in clear sky;
sponge-cake trees
tumble together into
verdant *vallate*
releasing rivulets
of mountain water.
Sole sailboat
drifts by,
its silhouette caught
in a Rosai dream.

Rosai: Ottone Rosai, Italian artist

Border Crossing, 1978

From *dogana*
black-clad *carabinieri*
with holstered hidden
gun, guard
Caesarean-split Chiasso
showing tri-colour ensign,
garrulous.

Sharing silver kiosk
grey-uniformed *polizia*
with concealed pistol
protect Swiss entry
red-white flag free
in neutral wind,
polite.

Memories of
watchtower and wire
partisan and Duce
are torn from
primal senses.

Country Inn

we desert Tokaido of carts and horn blasts
for dim corridor of screen world
flower urn simplicity and Shinto alcoves

a breeze announces
vegetable and fish delicacies
brought by kimono attendants
who leave us in delicate seclusion

retainers swirl room into lantern memories
soft light casts images
of feudal lords, calligraphers, statesmen
on parchment shades

we, the sole recipients
of fourteenth-generation hospitality
a walled interlude with time

Kyoto, 1980

The Field: Fourth Decade

they arrive for business disguised by breakfast
lieutenant with scribe staffman, concealed
in wool and shine polyester, western camouflage,
his English counterpart with rotund wife
snacks eggs and marmalade toast sticks;
disdaining culinary weaponry, they launch oratory
retool opponents' cogent data
disarm request for quantity considerations
dismantle fairness appeal,
silent secretary blitzes logic –
thrusts pre-drawn contracts

mercenaries withdraw, leaving chit unturned
field camouflage untouched
knife beside congealed eggs

Tokyo, 1980

Vienna Visit

I stalk cobble-sloped
stained stones
of Judenstrasse,
secured by plaster
walls with chiselled
cherub pediments,
to Stadttempel's brown
worn wooden doors;
above apartments
across craft shops
synagogue, as decreed,
dissolves into surroundings
sole survivor

gun-carrying *polizei*
guard square –
pacing, impatient, aloof
police car's pulsing scream
pumps conditioned chilled terror
into charred souls

centuries chanting cadence
of *mincha ma'ariv* begins

Vienna, 1979

Haifa, Israel

The city spreads below me
twinkling with millennia
of light.
Cinderella ships wait
admission as cargo carriers
transport life
into this port-fortress
under the frozen gaze
of the *Af ai pi chen.*
Soldiers secure
streets, orchards, and shrines
hoping for the West wind
and peace.

*Af ai pi chen: Hebrew, "notwithstanding." A boat used during the illegal
immigration period, now a naval museum in Haifa harbour.*

Kiryat Shmona, 1974

"Hello," the little voice sung,
Ambling best as he was able.
"That?" asked the small one
Finger pointing toward Passover table.

"Come, sit on my lap and we will begin."
Unleavened bread recalls the speed
From Pharaoh's land we had to leave.
Darling, do not fear the whine and spin.

"This, this?" the little voice asked.
With blood of paschal lamb upon our door
God's angel of death knew to pass o'er.
Darling, do not tremble at the blast.

"This" the son eagerly wanted to know.
Maror is for endless building under overseers.
Bitter herbs, for toil mixed with tears.
Darling, the time has come for me to go.

The boy looked wise from all he learned;
No longer a baby sound or cry
But a run, a fierce hug of goodbye.
Darling, I know not if I shall return.

Kiryat Shmona: an Israeli cooperative settlement across the Lebanese border

The Soldiers

They walk arm-in-arm
down the Roman steps
the blind soldier linked
to his armless friend
talking, laughing in Hebrew.
Behind, a wheelchair.
Another contorts
from shell-shock.
Tandem bicycles
rest against antiquity's
walls, ready for the
sightless.
They approach the
Roman ruins,
the deaf, blessed,
unable to hear
the pound of
Syrian guns.

Memorial at Golan Heights

Carved names cut
the granite
into black blood
and pour upon the
concrete ground.
The bunkers lie
bleak, dark, deserted
camouflaged by
rock and tree.
Barbed wire
warns where mines
still gnarl the land.

We will not forget
though sole swallow's cry
cuts the empty silence.

Dead Sea

Mountains pink and rounded
surround me
as I surrender
to the magic water.
Weightless I float
on a sea of salt
pushed by child's breath
to-and-fro,
rocked as in a dream
suspended
between the line
of belief and disbelief,
of peace and war.

Masada

The sun scours
the ancient rocks
baking its limestone
dust.
Birds weave over
reconstructed ruins
witnesses to time.
Silence, sweet and still
screams to be remembered
as skeletons of bravery
lie buried under
burnt stone –
children with mothers
men linked in faith.
Now paratroopers
march over crusty stone
and take their oath
to remember.

Valley of Jezreel

Armageddon,
you have called
out your warnings
to all nations
yet you lie laden
with fruits and cotton,
resting your bloodstained soil.
Saul, I hear your anguish
echo from mountain peaks
and sweet Deborah,
your trumpet's call.
Through the mist
shadows of French,
British, and Turks march
to the clash of drums.
But now rest,
sleeping Jezreel, rest.

The Guide

He drives his car
wherever they tell him
to Masada or Bethlehem,
Ben Yehuda or Hayarkam.
He jokes in five languages
English, Arabic, and Italian,
German when necessary.
He plays his cassette,
Goodman or Shaw
for his Americans
and Caruso for others.
He opens doors,
waits in marble lobbies,
explains history tirelessly.
In his pocket, a Gun
on his arm, a Number
in his heart, Steel.

The Cycle

[EDITOR'S NOTE: *Much of the poetry in this section is appearing in print for the first time. Written over a twenty year period, these poems capturing the stages in a family's life were purposely held by the author with the intention of presenting them as a unit.*]

Renoir Child

if I can own one memory
it is you, my Renoir child
that pastel garden morning
barefoot, upon an emerald carpet
brushed with sun
joyous, abandoned
sprinting a soft path
amidst the flower faces
and furry bumblebees

unaware of the artist's deft eye

For Tracy

she sleeps silently
face white from suspended motion
open lips touching tiny gnawed fist
mouth quivering with dreams;
how I wish rabbit and bunny sentinels
could ever protect you from an
age that rapes childhood
for competition and success,
where dreams waken into nightmare
and change becomes revolution;
sleep, sleep my little one
and when you wake, wake slowly

Butterfly

these are dandelion fields
and waves of yellow grass,
cocoon sails, sway secure
from rooted myrrh shoots;
my child, beauteous of soul
you are the world's sleeping occupant,
suspended between leaf and leaf
to tumble radiant
upon an awaiting world

Innocence

she plops into chill pepper sand
of shell babies and sea fantasies
chatters with beach wanderers
of family, stored dreams;
studies nesting egrets, bellies
dampening in tide cascades,
hears gull whimpers, straw whispers
wind drying cormorants' winged expanse

innocent of the bluefish
who shed the sea in pack hunger,
gnaw baitless lures with razor heat
and the ebb of gular breath
sucked from the white shattered sky giant
to vanish
in night's incessantly black sea-lunge

My Son

small, you nuzzled in my shoulder
frail frame taut
all motion, breath suspended
as my heart became yours

now we wander woodlands
caress fuzz shell of secret poppy
hiding parchment petals,
awaken to watch
a valley of sparkles blink
at the warm summer night;
in the place where flowers grow
you too grow
camouflaged by Blue Jay cap,
muscled limbs, gentle;
again you grasp my heart
renew belief and sustain my soul

The Question

your father's arm cradles questions
of history, heritage torn
from hand-scrawled death diaries,
war journals;
answers, prismed through
forties' black spectacles

your child eyes, luminate
disgorged human cattle cars
Nazi salutes
boy at crossing
holding hand of pince-nez father
unafraid, trusting
both waved to right
in slow procession to barracked death
cadenced to string quartet's
cultured camouflage-passion

I fight the image
blot my eyes
concentrate on soft father-son words
motor whine over silent lake
twilight's silk shadows
Canadian century rooted green:
for you are mine, my son,
my Jewish son,
and I do not know God's future

Nana

FOR IDA BERK

Grey hairs frame
silkened face
carved with lines of loving.
A gown drapes
her perfect posture, regal
in that worn-green chair
heirloom from a past
I touch only through
eyes of milked vision.
Ageless hands
caress picture-memories
then clasp mine
meaningfully:
my love-link to the future.

The World Builder

He stands no taller
than the stalks of grass
red shirt flagging green,
studying the bang, banging.

A terrier
comes to his side
rubs lovingly against him.
Poised, alert on toes
he never moves;
this world builder.

The Nurturer

wind laps summer silk
while you dream
beside buttercups
scented Queen Anne's lace

child limbs sprawl upon me
raspberry stained fingers limp
fragile frame slackens
sleep-rhythmed heart draws close

again placenta bound,
now you, sweet slumberer
are the nurturer
and I, the sustained

Transition

they stand as one
gazing at the centre of the universe
souls touching

they rejoin life,
ambition under necessity's guise
parties, pressure, applause;
gone the quiet times
of lingering talk
and gentle laughter

each alone
beyond the centre of the universe
they wonder

Lake Counterpoint

I

century cedar leaves curl
pale green underbelly raw
birch twigs twist, snap
their sapling stems anguished
hammock tree-belly taut, contorts;
gull and island slab
lunge in convulse wash,
speed creatures dart
for swollen sanctuary,
rain pellets assault earth;
sky-fire crackles

II

seagulls slide across
silvered stream, voices
screech to sky brothers
across bay, boat engine
splices stilled water,
its whine dissolves;
a wind-breath ruffles lake
laps its cool liquid
over ivory stones;
the children's laughter skips
and lingers

Beach Day

toddler crab crawls
onto slick water cot
appended to perfect pedicured toes
then rests dimpled cheeks
on freshly waxed legs
triumphant,
man paces winter-bruised dock
surveys tempest spat glass
diet trunks bulging,
boys, raft-Jedis
sprawl slender youth frames
across bobbing star-craft island
gull decorated in
polka-dot wash,
family cat sleeps in
swollen heat
beneath fat August maple
on stuffed cushion
whiskered mouth smiling

The Generation Gap

I've seen fields far greener than theirs
travelling miles to liberated schools
that spun sex education with co-ed dorms
rejecting privileged sororities and old school ties.

And now degree laden, desires achieved
I find my hope for the future
as did my parents before me
in the faces of my sleeping young.

Stages

you curl into my body
in this magic room, still so small,
tender hands again clasp mine,
a sweet embrace

we, unlike the Lilliputians have grown
you fearless in limb and mind;
I now weaker
tremble before dragons

I can only warm danger
wrap you in love
and cheer, as you
sinewed with dreams, stride

Garden

in this garden
walled by love
with books, plenteous
as field flowers
we chatter, two friends
our thoughts birthed
one from the other
of all that matters
in the universe

Resemblance to Anne

my darling's eyes
mirror hers
deep and caring,
her coral voice
tumbles the wind,
limbs sprawl among books

but how to forget
the train-children:
skeletons of small bones
emaciated faces
riddled with trust
that stare in shadows of my night?

Father-Son

they weave through picnic carnage
and the sleepy people
protective, the boy guides father to Sunday lake
together, they tumble the water
freed in porpoise play

then rest, hands entwined –
boy releases secret fears
man strokes honeyed skin, child curls
and oblivious to boat whine
the drift of time, strenghtened they dream

Holding Back Time

under ruffle buds, we sit
beside last season's dock
each stone, a prism jewel
cloud princesses wisp upon seagull charioteers
a bud drops its protective skin

we cling heartbeats close
caught, between spring's fleeting
summer's bloom
and trying vainly, desperately
to stay the illusion

Friend

how can I forget
when in daily life
your name slips from my lips
naturally, as sunshine

I seek places you have seen
friends that were yours
draw strength in recalling
even now, things you have said

lilacs scent the spring air
chestnuts fall from ripened leaves
in your tiny city garden,
season touches season

and I remember
a man of compassion
you caught my life and held it sacred
as I do your memory

Sounds

I heard the children listening
as the brass ensemble began to play
in that chalk-dusted school,
heard the silence between the notes
that swirled and tumbled round the room,
heard the hushed breath of the youth
chin resting on numbed hand
heard a faint hum from the girl
perched on reddened knees,
Greek, Italian, Portuguese;
heard sounds created from
instruments never seen before.
Today I heard the sounds of learning
and I put away all fear.

Spring Grass

pictures pull back
memories of cut grass
thrown about
like green confetti
settling softly
again on spring soil

I think of your
face, my son, eager
laughing at that
spring grass,
your eyes
innocent and clear,
hands reaching
for the future

Rite of Passage

they share a tender journey
across a threshold I dare not follow
with knowing smiles, fraternal hugs
requests for private talks
the son, always caring of the father

from a distance, I watch
the uncertain youth form the man
and recall, the quiet season
my joy in you
grateful for your ever gentle soul

Memorial Service

Sitting in this quiet place
memory returns to my
picture of you and grandpa
that last summer,
arms linked, trousered,
happy beside your garden.
Hearing your name called
I know why I am here
though all I can recall is that picture.
I am part of you,
and my children
hushed, unknowing beside me,
carry you and your love in them.

A Special Season

We walk on coral carpet sand;
air-suspended osprey snatch
squashed child crusts
and surround hand clapping siblings,
satiated wind birds rest
preen salted feathers with beak thrusts;
soft footprints linger on chipped shell-shore

We watch from the tall grass;
ocean mouth froths till air foam
twists down rag-tattered beach
raped of cone-clustered treasures
and covered turtle eggs,
of coon oysters cultivating in
mangrove's tangled thickets;
sea-grape splatters its bittersweet syrup

We fish in wind-soaked mud slicks;
snowy pelicans cling to whipped pine
white dots hinge to evergreen
to plummet, through Christmas chilled sky,
snook and tarpon stalk shallower shelters,
slide into crane canals;
a beached sea trout struggles, strains

We linger beside the brackish lagoon
anhinga arch necks in subaqua snake dance
and spear fish with swift bill-bayonet
surface, shake webbed feet;
roseate spoonbill belly-bobbing on stilts

stir, stalk mud shallows
with fat spatulated clamp;
duckweed webs encircle life's moist roots

We study from torn anthologies
of Caloosa's sand-shell village society,
Ponce de Leon's fatal arrow slash
and fables of female prisoners, pirate brigands;
the chilled sun flamed into eclipse

And we spoke always of the grandmother
gracious, gentle, blessed in memory
who left us with one
silent, shattering heart skip

Adolescence

trusting, the eyes
and the smile that quivers tenuously
until reciprocated
ripens into the blush of a single dimple

kind, the thoughts
unblemished by pain
a mind cultivated by compassion
and volumed books
their home succulent and savoured

impatient, the intellect
the "why not" and "can't we"
questions that pry at essence
their core, sensitive as her own
with will to 'tempt a better generation

Time, grow gentle
on this tender being
nudge her, softly
along the fragile journey

The Lesson

I take you with me
as a heartbeat
tucked inside my soul
into the backstreets

for you, will ask questions
the reason ghetto birthed
across trade canals
who slept in the dungeons of Europe
beneath the shadow spires of Christ
the need to climb tiers
to the sanctuary of synagogue

and will not accept Their answers
a curt dismissal, the averted eye
but probe, an innocent's voice
the reason
and wise, blaze it to memory

The Zenith

at the zenith, you stride
muscled and lean
the mocha sand firms
beneath your feet
a pleasing gait to be chased
but never again caught by me

walk we two this birthing place
this genesis
towards the closing horizon
and share the myriad thoughts
questions that toss, exposed
the dream treasures coaxed
from a keen mind

the sea shatters and subsides
—lush the harvest
my son, my companion, my friend

When I Must Go 'Way

when I must go 'way
what can I leave to soothe
when wind burdens your back
hurts afflict your vulnerable heart
life jabs a random, jocular blow?

how to remind you of my love
the link of one heart to another
my certainty
in your strong, sensitive self
its ability to withstand

what can I leave
when words
once my ally, slip away?

Remembering

often we have come here
where leaves grow mammoth green
elms shimmer, shelter while you ride
a magic mammal
festive fin waving high

I return with passing seasons
to this emerald slope, alone
stumble through high grass
over a crusted waking form

through memory of hugs and laughter
the touch of summer's gleam
splendid, the plastic porpoise
beckons with the stir of sand and dreams

Renewal

FOR MAX

To beginnings, we return
this wondrous country
where we pledged, each to the other
our lifetimes

our transport
a sequence of memory
the tender years,
sweet and caring

from a distance, repeats
a splatter of gardenia, delicate and fragrant

as gardeners replenish beds
confident in the season's bloom
I recall it all
that it lives and grows
and remains, my forever.

Genesis

We are back
at the beginning again
you and I and the tree
where all has been given to us
even each other
in an enchanted playground
and nothing but time,
endless time to learn
the truth we lost.

The previously published poems in this collection have been selected from:

THROUGH THE EYES OF A WOMAN (1975): *The Age of Aquarius, Bon Voyage, Canadian Paradox, City Spring, Dawn, Dossier, Earthquake, Elegy for a Starfish, For Tracy, From North Bay, The Generation Gap, Genesis, He, Homecoming, I'm Alive Again, In-flight, Kiryat Shmona 1974, The Legacy, The Master, Memorial Service, Northern Morning, Peace with Honour, The Predator, The Race, Recycled History, Remembrance Day, Rummage Sale, Site Plan for Subdivision A, Sounds, Spring Fog, Stroke, Susan's Story, Tuesday's Rape, Transition, The Victim, Visit to the Ottawa, Waste, While New York Burns, The World Builder, The Wrecking.*

TAKING OFF (1979): *Autumn, Awakening, The Bat, Bermuda, Border Crossing 1978, City-State 1978, Columbia Icefields, The Conquerors, Cretan Fisherman, Dead Sea, The Deer, Elounda Night, Escorted Inclusive Tour, Farm Winter, Gandria Morning, The Grand Hotel Villa D'Este, Greatness, The Guide, Haifa Israel, Ice-Mountain, Images in Snow, St. John, Journey's End, Kingdom of Mycenae, Lake Scene, Malpensa Italy, Marking Time, Masada, Meaning, Memorial at Golan Heights, Nana, Outdoor Tea-Time, Port of Piraeus Greece, Prayer in Distomon, Sint Maarten/St. Martin, Siren's Lure, The Soldiers, Spring Grass, The Swimmer, Temple of Poseidon at Cape Sounion, Valley of Jezreel, View from a Hill, The Visitor, Winter Ride.*

CHINA: SHOCKWAVES (1987): *Aftershock, The Ambassador to Beijing, As If They Had Never Been, Awareness, Bargain, Beach Day, Block Captain, The Bond, Carousel, China Trader, The Choice, Chungking Incursion, Commune Visits, Country Inn, Decision, East Is Red Steamer, English Teacher Foreign Language Institute, Exile, The Field: Fourth Decade, Foreign Concessions 1980s, From Victoria Peak, The Gathering, Glass Brothers, Great Hall of the People, The Great Wall of China, Hong Kong Skyline, Impasse, Innocence, Lake Counterpoint, Lake Tai Images, The Lesson, Li River Cruise, Moods (from a balcony), Ming Tombs, Overnight in Shanghai, Peninsula Lobby, Power, The Question, Resemblance to Anne, The Reunion, A Special Season, Tiananmen Square, Vienna Visit, View from Catching Cloud Pavilion, Visit to Thirteenth Middle School, Wan Xian, Xing Guo Guest House, Yangtze River Gorges.*

NANCY-GAY ROTSTEIN *has been internationally praised for her poetry which includes the collections* Through the Eyes of a Woman *(1975),* Taking Off *(1979) and* China: Shockwaves *(1987). She is also the author of a critically acclaimed first novel,* Shattering Glass *(1997), which has been published in Canada and the United States and translated into eight languages. Nancy-Gay Rotstein received an M.A. in history from the University of Toronto. She holds an LL.B. from Osgoode Hall Law School and is a member of the Ontario Bar. She has been appointed to the Board of Directors of the Canada Council, the National Library and Telefilm Canada. She lives near Toronto.*